**Spotlight on Kids Can Code**

# Understanding Coding with

# JAVA

**Emilee Hillman**

**PowerKiDS** press

New York

Published in 2018 by The Rosen Publishing Group, Inc.
29 East 21st Street, New York, NY 10010

Copyright © 2018 by The Rosen Publishing Group, Inc.

All rights reserved. No part of this book may be reproduced in any form without permission in writing from the publisher, except by a reviewer.

First Edition

Editor: Elizabeth Krajnik
Book Design: Michael J. Flynn

Photo Credits: Cover Mari/E+/Getty Images; p. 5 Izabela Habur/E+/Getty Images; p. 7 Ekaterina_Minaeva/Shutterstock.com; p. 8 Christopher Meder/Shutterstock.com; p. 15 Bobicova Valeria/Shutterstock.com; p. 17 Mauro Saivezzo/Shutterstock.com; p. 19 Yui Mok/AP Images; p. 20 toozdesign/Shutterstock.com; p. 22 Gil C/Shutterstock.com.

The LEGO name and products, including MINDSTORMS and WeDo, are trademarks of the LEGO Group, and their use in this book does not imply a recommendation or endorsement of this title by the LEGO Group.

Minecraft is a trademark of Mojang (a game development studio owned by Microsoft Technology Corporation), and its use in this book does not imply a recommendation or endorsement of this title by Mojang or Microsoft.

Cataloging-in-Publication Data

Names: Hillman, Emilee.
Title: Understanding coding with Java / Emilee Hillman.
Description: New York : PowerKids Press, 2018. | Series: Spotlight on kids can code | Includes index.
Identifiers: ISBN 9781508155263 (pbk.) | ISBN 9781508155140 (library bound) | ISBN 9781508154792 (6 pack)
Subjects: LCSH: Java (Computer program language) | Application software–Development.
Classification: LCC QA76.73.J38 H55 2018 | DDC 005.13'3–dc23

Manufactured in the United States of America

CPSIA Compliance Information: Batch #BS17PK: For Further Information contact Rosen Publishing, New York, New York at 1-800-237-9932

# Contents

Introduction to Java.....................4

What Is Java?..........................6

Learn the Rules.......................8

Getting Started.......................10

Fundamentals.........................12

Variables and Data Types...........14

Hello World!..........................16

Java and *Minecraft*..................18

Java Programs........................20

Good Programming....................22

Glossary..............................23

Index.................................24

Websites.............................24

# Introduction to Java

Imagine you're walking down the toy aisle trying to choose what toy you want for your birthday. There are so many choices! How will you decide which one to buy? When choosing a programming language to use, there are almost as many choices as there are toys in the toy store. You might think of Java as a toy car. You can find a toy car in any toy store and Java is one of the most common programming languages.

Java is not only used to create programs on the Internet but also a variety of smartphone **applications**. Java is used to create most Android applications. You may be surprised how many devices and applications you encounter every day run with the help of Java. However, if you try Java and it isn't your favorite programming language, there are many others to choose from.

Choosing a programming language can be hard when there are so many options. Consider what you'd like to create and choose from the programming languages that best fit the job.

# What Is Java?

Java is an object-oriented programming (OOP) language, which means it focuses on objects. Objects in Java are similar to physical items in real life. These objects can be named, described, changed, and used in different ways. When you write a program in Java, you start with naming an object within a class and then decide what to do with it from there.

Coding with Java is a little like building with a LEGO kit. In a new LEGO kit, you get lots of different pieces, which are like Java objects. An object's state is what it's like. In the same way, LEGO bricks may have different colors or different numbers of studs.

Object behaviors are represented as **methods** or **functions**. Some LEGO bricks can be used to make things move or create a more stable construction. In the same way, objects can do different things and behave in different ways depending on their methods or functions.

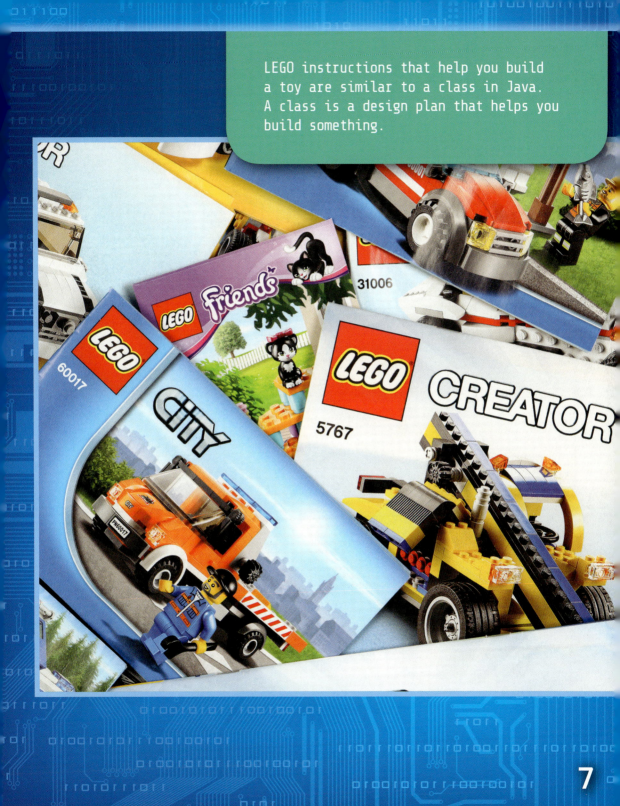

LEGO instructions that help you build a toy are similar to a class in Java. A class is a design plan that helps you build something.

# Learn the Rules

Before you can begin using a programming language or writing code, you need to know that computer programming is about following rules. Knowing these rules will help you create a program that runs without errors. They will also help other programmers read and understand your programs.

**Rule 1:** Coders must know what they want the computer to do and write a plan.

**Rule 2:** Coders must use special words called **commands** to have the computer accept **input**, make choices, and take action.

**Rule 3:** Coders need to think about what tasks can be put into a group.

**Rule 4:** Coders need to employ **logic** using AND, OR, NOT, and other key words.

**Rule 5:** Coders must explore the **environment** and understand how it works.

Once you understand these rules, you'll be ready to learn more about Java and other programming languages.

# Getting Started

The first step for learning Java is setting up your environment. You can use a text editor or an integrated development environment (IDE). An IDE is software in which you can write your programs and practice running them. One advantage of some IDEs is that you can use **tutorials**. Some IDEs can check your work with testing and **diagnostic** tools, which act like spell check for programmers.

You also need to make sure you have downloaded Java Development Kit (JDK) to your computer. JDK is free to download for any platform. After you start a new project, make sure you name it carefully to reflect what you want to do, use the **file extension** ".java", and save it.

You can use a number of different text editors and IDEs to create a program using Java. Some popular free IDEs are NetBeans, Eclipse, and Komodo Edit.

*Eclipse*

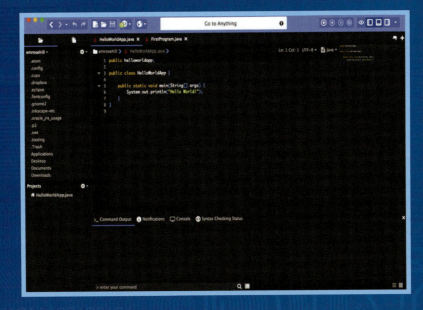

*Komodo Edit 10*

# Fundamentals

Like learning a new spoken language, learning a programming language can be difficult. However, if you break it down into parts, you will see how those parts fit together to make a program.

Java code is made up of a combination of letters, numbers, and other characters. The order of these elements is very important. Each character must be in the correct order for your program to run properly. Any mistakes in your code will produce errors. It is good practice to always check your work, just like you would for a math problem.

When you start a new project, the first thing to do is create a class. A class describes how objects (such as letters, words, and numbers) will behave. Java has some classes that are already created, but you can also create your own.

## Breaking the Code

Java uses white space to make code easier to read and to group together parts of code that are related. White space is just what it sounds like—any blank space where you do not see characters. White space is created using spaces, tabs, and enter/return. Java knows to ignore this white space and focus on the commands in the code. There are some rules about where to put space and how much space to use between certain parts of a program. However, a program will run with or without white space.

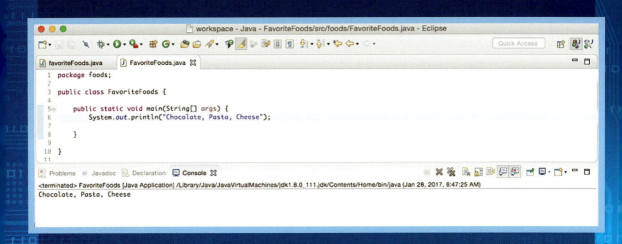

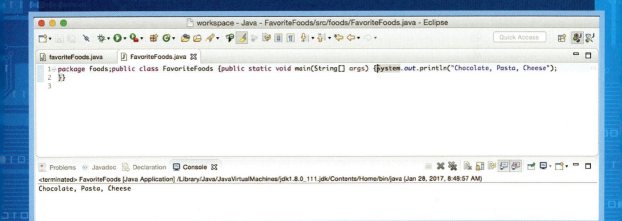

This is a simple program that will print out a list of foods. The first image has white space to separate each part of the program. The second doesn't have white space. Both programs will run and print, as can be seen from the System.out.println("Chocolate, Pasta, Cheese"); code. However, the program with white space is much easier to read because of the separation between each line of the program.

# Variables and Data Types

A **variable** is where objects or information is placed. This information can be letters, numbers, or other characters. To use a variable in your program, you have to give it a name first (such as "tax") and then define it with a **data type**.

When working with numbers, you use the data types "int," "long," "float," and "double." The data type "int," which is short for "interger," is used for smaller whole numbers. The data type "long" is used for very large whole numbers; "float" is used for numbers with a decimal point; and "double" is used for very large numbers with a decimal point.

If we want our program to calculate the cost of an item with sales tax added, we might use a variable named "tax" and the variable data type "float."

> Java's many different variables store information. Some of the most basic variables in Java are know as primitives. These include "byte," "short," "int," "long," "float," "double," "char," and "boolean."

# Breaking the Code

When naming variables, you need to write the names without spaces. Programmers use naming systems such as CamelCase or snake_case instead of spaces between the words in their variable names. CamelCase uses uppercase letters for each word like humps on a camel. Snake_case uses an underscore to connect words. It's important to remember exactly how you name your variables and programs because they won't run if you don't type them with the same uppercase and lowercase letters you used to create them.

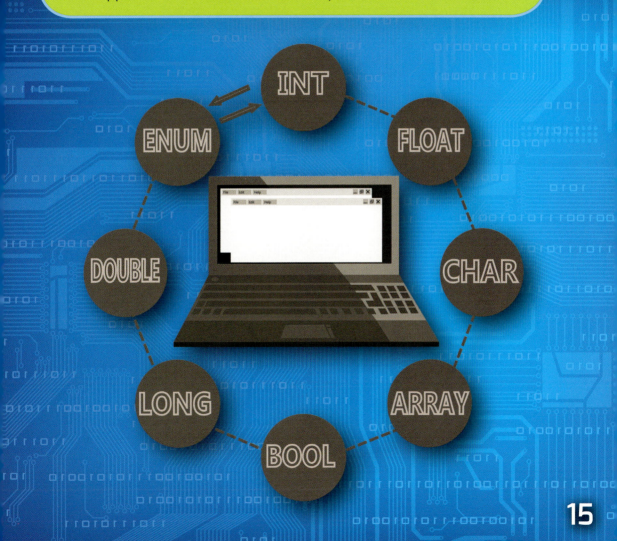

# Hello World!

Hello World is a basic program that tells the computer to print, or display, the text "Hello world!" To write this program, you first have to create a new project in your IDE or text editor and name your project "HelloWorld.java".

Next, you will create a class that explains the purpose of your program. Then, write out your main method, which is the first line of code that is executed when the program is run. The main method in Java is like a list of things to do. The following words are always used in the main method: "public static void main(String [ ] args) {." The last line of this program is a print line, which tells the computer to print the words "Hello world!" one time for each time the program is run. This means the words will be typed out on the screen or terminal where the program is being run.

```java
public class HelloWorld {

    public static void main(String[] args) {
        System.out.println("Hello world!");

    }

}
```

HelloWorld.java

Problems  @ Javadoc  Declaration  Console

<terminated> HelloWorld [Java Application] /Library/Java/JavaVirtualMachines/jdk1.8.0_111.jdk/Contents/Ho
Hello world!

This "Hello World" program is written in Eclipse. The line "System.out.println("Hello world!");" is the main method that will print the line of text "Hello world!" in the console.

# Java and *Minecraft*

Java is easier to understand than some programming languages and can be used on computers, gaming systems, smartphones, and tablets. Because it's one of the most popular programming languages, it's widely used to create web and desktop applications and design games such as *Minecraft*.

*Minecraft* is a popular sandbox construction game created using Java. This type of game allows users freedom to make decisions about where to go and what to do. Java was a good programming language to use to create *Minecraft* because it's easy to use with different computer operating systems, such as Windows, macOS, and Linux. *Minecraft* is also available on some gaming systems and pocket gaming devices, but those versions were written with C++ programming language.

*Minecraft* is just one example of a real-world application of Java.

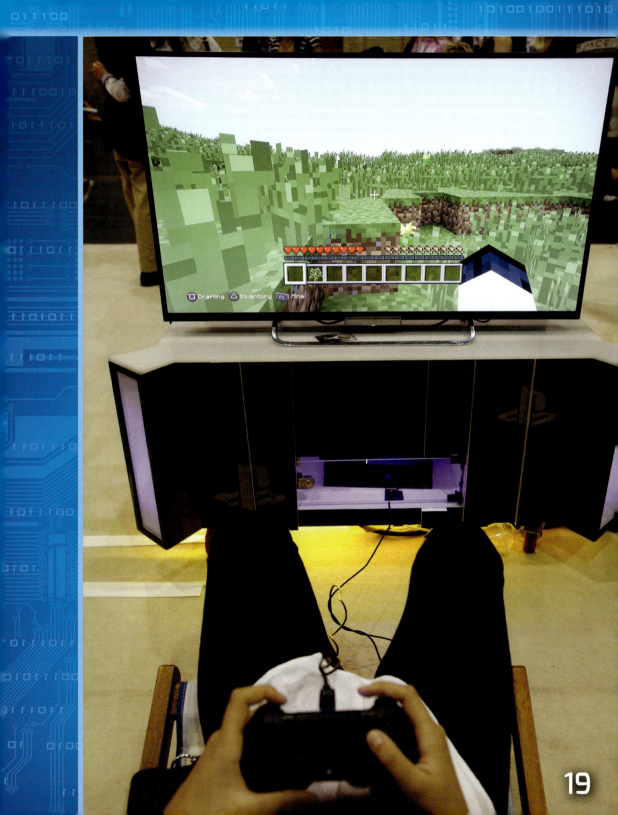

# Java Programs

Once you create your first program, you may start to wonder what other programs you can create using Java. Some of the most basic programs you can create with Java can store information and do math operations. You can save a person's name after they type it into your program. You can create a program to add up your purchases and then calculate the tax if you're purchasing something in an application.

Another type of program follows certain steps when conditions are met. When you are playing a game, you might be collecting coins to level up. That program is waiting for certain conditions to be met in order to run another line of code.

# Java Data Types

**boolean:** used for true and false data only

**byte:** used for smaller numbers from -128 to 127

**char:** used for a single character, like a letter or a symbol

**double:** used for very large numbers with decimal points

**float:** used for numbers that have a decimal point

**int:** a data type used for numbers ranging from -2,147,483,648 to 2,147,483,647

**long:** a data type used for numbers ranging from 9,223,372,036,854,775,808 to 9,223,372,036,854,755,807

**short:** used for slightly larger numbers from -32,768 to 32,767

# Java Math Operations

**\*** used for multiplication

**/** used for division

**%** used for division with a remainder

**+** used for addition

**-** used for subtraction

**==** used when two numbers are equal

**=!** used when two numbers are unequal

**<** used when the first number is less than

**>** used when the first number is greater than

**<=** used when the first number is less than or equal to

**>=** used when the first number is greater than or equal to

These data types and variables will help you understand and master Java.

# Good Programming

When creating a program with Java, make sure you add comments. Comments supply programmers with information about the program they want to run, such as the name of its creator or what the code does. Comments will be helpful to you and to anyone who might want to use one of your programs. You can easily add comments to your program by starting a line with "//."

Good programmers know that sometimes programs don't work on the first try. If you practice writing programs and read through other people's programs, you'll get better.

Many different companies all over the world use Java because it can be used to create many different things and is easy to use. Learning Java is a great way to begin a career in computer science.

22

# Glossary

**application:** A software program that runs on a computer, smartphone, tablet, or web browser.

**command:** A code or message that tells a computer to do something.

**data type:** The type of data that can be stored in a variable.

**diagnostic:** Used to locate issues in a program.

**environment:** The combination of computer hardware and software that allows a user to perform various tasks.

**file extension:** The letters and numbers that make up the last part of a file name, such as .docx or .txt.

**function:** Part of a program that performs a specific task.

**input:** Information that is put into a computer.

**logic:** A proper or reasonable way of thinking about or understanding something.

**method:** A procedure, or list of tasks, associated with a class.

**tutorial:** A book or guided program that provides information about a specific topic.

**variable:** A placeholder value that can change depending on conditions or other information passed to the program.

# Index

**A**
Android, 4

**C**
C++, 18
CamelCase, 15
class, 6, 7, 12, 16
commands, 9, 12
comments, 22

**D**
data typc, 14, 21

**E**
Eclipse, 10, 11, 17
environment, 9, 10

**F**
functions, 6

**I**
integrated development environment (IDE), 10, 16

**J**
Java Development Kit (JDK), 10

**K**
Komodo Edit, 10, 11

**L**
LEGO, 6, 7
Linux, 18
logic, 9

**M**
macOS, 18
methods, 6, 16, 17
*Minecraft*, 18

**N**
NetBeans, 10

**O**
object-oriented programming (OOP), 6
objects, 6, 12, 14

**P**
primitives, 14

**S**
snake_case, 15
state, 6

**T**
text editor, 10, 16

**V**
variables, 14, 15, 21

**W**
Windows, 18

# Websites

Due to the changing nature of Internet links, PowerKids Press has developed an online list of websites related to the subject of this book. This site is updated regularly. Please use this link to access the list: www.powerkidslinks.com/skcc/java